FUNNY JOKES FOR 8 YEAR OLD KIDS

100+ Crazy Jokes That Will Make You Laugh Out Loud!

Cooper the Pooper

© Copyright 2021 Cooper the Pooper - All rights reserved.

The content contained within this book may not be reproduced, duplicated or transmitted without direct written permission from the author or the publisher.

Under no circumstances will any blame or legal responsibility be held against the publisher, or author, for any damages, reparation or monetary loss due to the information contained within this book, either directly or indirectly.

Legal Notice:

This book is copyright protected. It is only for personal use. You cannot amend, distribute, sell, use, quote or paraphrase any part, or the content within this book, without the consent of the author or publisher.

Disclaimer Notice:

Please note the information contained within this document is for educational and entertainment purposes only. All effort has been executed to present accurate, up to date, reliable, complete information. No warranties of any kind are declared or implied. Readers acknowledge that the author is not engaged in the rendering of legal, financial, medical or professional advice. The content within this book has been derived from various sources. Please consult a licensed professional before attempting any techniques outlined in this book.

By reading this document, the reader agrees that under no circumstances is the author responsible for any losses, direct or indirect, that are incurred as a result of the use of the information contained within this document, including, but not limited to, errors, omissions or inaccuracies.

TABLE OF CONTENTS

Table of Contents 3

Introduction 4

Chapter 1: Funny Jokes 6

Chapter 2: Crazy Jokes 18

Chapter 3: Laugh-out-Loud Jokes 30

Chapter 4: Knock-Knock Jokes 42

Chapter 5: Bonus Jokes 54

Final Words 66

INTRODUCTION

There is nothing better than getting to school with some new jokes ready to tell your friends.

I mean, making people laugh — it is the best.

Seriously, the best.

Which is actually the reason I decided to write this book in the first place.

When I was a puppy, I just loved telling jokes. Every weekend I would spend hours upon hours looking for new jokes that I could share with my friends and family. Jokes that would have them rolling around on the ground as soon as they heard the punchline.

But the thing was, for every good joke I heard, there were ten bad ones.

In short, I thought the kids of the world needed a book of jokes where every single one was funny — a book like this one, for example.

I have spent the last few years searching the world for the funniest jokes on the planet. I have looked high and low for the best jokes I could find, all so I could put them in a book — this book, to be precise.

In your hand you hold a book of the best jokes in the world, designed specifically for eight-year-old kids. The jokes in this book are so good they will have you wishing you could stop laughing (not that you will be able to).

And it gets even better.

I have found that the jokes in this book get funnier the more you share them. Which means that you should take the time to remember your favorites so you can share them with your friends and family.

So, what are you waiting for? Turn the first page and start reading the funniest jokes for eight-year-old kids on the planet.

1

Where are sharks originally from?

- Finland.

2

What do cats love to eat for breakfast?

- Mice Krispies.

3

Why are skeletons evil?

- They are heartless!

4

Where did the fox go when it lost its tail?

- A retail store!

(5)

What kind of bees eat flesh?

- Zombees.

(6)

How does a cucumber become a pickle?

- It goes through a jarring experience.

What is a bear with no ear called?

• B.

Why did the banana go to the doctor?

• It wasn't peeling well.

9

What is a Martian's favorite chocolate?

- **A Mars bar!**

10

Where do you learn greetings?

- **At hi-school.**

How did one candle tease the other?

• I'm going out tonight!

Something goes on and on and has an "i" in the middle. It also makes you cry. What is it?

• An onion.

13

What's common between elephants, trees, and cars?

- **They all have trunks!**

14

Why do the French love to eat snails?

- **They're not fast food.**

A monkey, a chipmunk, and a skunk decided to race to the top of a coconut tree. Who got the banana first: the monkey, the chipmunk, or the skunk?

- **None of them! It's a coconut tree! No bananas there!**

What do you call a dead snowman?

- **A puddle.**

Why was Dracula sick?
- **Because of his coffin.**

Why couldn't the bees catch the bus?
- **They missed the buzz stop.**

19

Why should you not let a bear operate the remote?

- **He will keep pressing the paws button.**

20

What's gray and goes around and around?

- **An elephant in a washing machine.**

Why did the cookie go to the hospital?

- Because he felt crummy.

What is the least spoken language in the world?

- Sign language.

CHAPTER 2
CRAZY JOKES

1

Did you hear what the judge said when the skunk walked into the courtroom?

- **Odor in the court!**

2

How do you have to wake up Lady Gaga?

- **Poker face.**

3

What gifts are Santa giving out this year?

- Santa-tizers.

4

Three people were sailing. All three fell off the boat. Only two ended up with their hair wet, but the third's stayed dry. Why?

- He was bald!

5

What position does Dracula like to play in baseball?

- **Bat!**

6

Where do you enjoy shopping?

- **At the satis-factory.**

What's the antonym of a restaurant?

- **A workaurant.**

What is bigger than Santa but much lighter than him?

- **His shadow.**

9

What do elves eat for breakfast?

- **Frosted Flakes.**

10

What's a royal pardon?

- **What the queen says after burping.**

What do you like most about Switzerland?

- **I don't know much about Switzerland, but the flag is a big plus!**

What is green but smells like yellow paint?

- **Green paint.**

13

What did the birthday cake say to the knife?

- You wanna piece of me?

14

Why do you never see elephants hiding in trees?

- Because they are really good at it.

15

Yesterday a man threw a glass of milk at me. What did I do?

- I thought, "How dairy!"

16

What did the potato say, before getting skinned?

- What did the potato say, before getting skinned?

17

What do you get if you cross a cheetah with a burger?

- Fast food.

18

What did the calculator say to the math student?

- You can count on me.

19

Why can't you trust zookeepers?

- **They love cheetahs.**

20

What time do you go to the dentist?

- **At tooth-hurty.**

21

Why did the leaf go to the doctor?

- **It was feeling green.**

22

Who did the scary ghost invite to his party?

- **Any old friend he could dig up!**

CHAPTER 3
LAUGH-OUT-LOUD JOKES

1

Why don't koalas count as bears?

- They don't have the right koalafications.

2

What's the biggest moth in the world?

- A mam-moth!

3

What does Dracula like to watch on TV?

- **Neck-flix!**

4

Why did the ghost go to the hair salon?

- **To make herself boo-tiful!**

5

What kind of guitar always has a cold?

- **An achoo-stic.**

6

What did the candle say to the envelope?

- **Seal you later.**

7

How did the mobile phone propose to his girlfriend?

- **He gave her a ring.**

8

Why did the puppy sit in the sun?

- **He wanted to be a hot dog!**

9

Why don't dinosaurs eat clowns?

- **Because they taste funny.**

10

Why was the principal so worried?

- **There were too many rulers at school.**

11

What's the best place to grow flowers in school?

• In kinder-garden.

12

What did the duck say to the waiter?

• Put it on my bill.

13

Why did the kid bring a ladder to school?

- Because he wanted to go to high school.

14

What toy is always in the bathroom?

- The TOY-let!

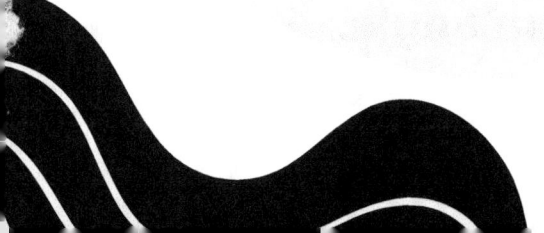

Why did the credit card go to jail?

- It was guilty as charged.

Why couldn't the student finish the geometry problem?

- She didn't look at it from a different angle.

17

Did you hear about the monster who ate too many houses?

- **Yes, he was homesick!**

18

Why did the laptop get glasses?

- **To improve its web sight.**

19

What do you call a boat that has a hole on the bottom?

- **A sink.**

20

Why do candles always go on the top of cakes?

- **Because it's hard to light them from the bottom.**

21

Where do library books like to sleep?

• **Under their covers!**

22

Why does underwear last longer than any other clothing?

• **Because it's never worn out.**

Knock, knock!
Who's there?
Rick.
Rick who?
Rick or treat?

Knock, knock!
Who's there?
Asphalt.
Asphalt who?
It's asphalt, not mine!

3

Knock, knock!

Who's there?
Maida.

Maida who?
Maida force be with you!

4

Knock, knock!

Who's there?
Italy.

Italy who?
Italy be a big job!

5

Knock, knock!

Who's there?

Interrupting me.

Int... who?

Dooooooooooon't.

6

Knock, knock!

Who's there?

Anny.

Anny who?

Anny-who, you want this pizza or not?

7

Knock, knock!

Who's there?
Israel.

Israel who?
Israel nice to meet you!

8

Knock, knock!

Who's there?
Albert.

Albert who?
Albert you can't guess who this is!

9

Knock, knock!

Who's there?
Harry.

Harry
Harry up. I need to pee!

10

Knock, knock!

Who's there?
A broken pencil.

A broken pencil who?
Never mind...it's pointless!

Knock, knock!

Who's there?

Francis.

Francis who?

France is a country in Europe.

Knock, knock!

Who's there?

Tennis.

Tennis who?

Tennis five plus five.

13

Knock, knock!
Who's there?
Water.

Water who?
Water you doing here?

14

Knock, knock!
Who's there?
Amos.

Amos who?
A mosquito bit me!

15

Knock, knock!

Who's there?
Alec.

Alec who?
Alec-tricity! Isn't that a shock!

16

Knock, knock!

Who's there?
Alfred.

Alfred who?
Alfred of the dark!

17

Knock, knock!
Who's there?
Sacha.

Sacha who?
Sacha lot of questions!

18

Knock, knock!
Who's there?
Sam.

Sam who?
Sam day you'll recognize me!

19

Knock, Knock!

Who's there?
Sara.

Sara who?
Sara 'nother way in?

20

Knock, Knock!

Who's there?
Shirley.

Shirley who?
Shirley you must know me by now!

21

Knock, knock!

Who's there?
Juno.

Juno who?
Juno I love you, right?

22

Knock, knock!

Who's there?
Celeste.

Celeste who?
Celeste time I lend you money!

1

Which is faster: cold or heat?

- Heat is; you can catch a cold.

2

What happened to the two comedians who got married?

- They lived happily ever "laughter!"

3

What do you call it when a really skinny person visits Hawaii?

- **A TOO WEAK** vacation.

Why didn't the invisible man accept the job offer?

- **He just couldn't see himself working there.**

Why did the man put sugar under his pillow?

- **So he would have sweet dreams.**

What did one volcano say to the other?

- **I lava you!**

What did the big flower say to the little flower?

- Hi, bud!

What was wrong with the wooden car?

- It wooden go!

Have you ever tried to eat a clock?

- No; it's very time consuming.

Why does Humpty Dumpty love autumn?

- Because he always has a great fall.

11

What did the tree say to the wind?

- Leaf me alone!

12

What do you call a fairy that doesn't like to shower?

- Stinkerbell.

(13)

What do skeletons say before a meal?

- "Bone appetite."

(14)

Why are circles so smart?

- Because they have 360 degrees.

15

On which side of the house do pine trees grow?

- **On the outside.**

16

What is the color of the wind?

- **Blew.**

(17)

What falls in winter but never gets hurt?

• Snow!

(18)

Why couldn't the pirate play cards?

• Because he was sitting on the deck.

19

Why did the burglar enter the singing contest?

- **He wanted to steal the show.**

20

How do you scare a snowman?

- **Show him a hair dryer.**

FINAL WORDS

Thank you so much for taking the time to read my book.

Writing this book was a massive effort. I spent over ten years traveling the globe looking for jokes that were funny enough to be in this book — and nothing makes me happier than knowing that great kids like you are reading them.

But remember, you are not finished yet.

Although you did make it to the end of the book, really, you're only just getting started.

Now you need to go back through the pages and pick out your favorite jokes so you can share them with your friends and family — after all, the only thing better than hearing a funny joke is telling a funny joke.

So, what are you waiting for — head back to the start of this book and prepare to share some laughs with everyone you know!

www.ingramcontent.com/pod-product-compliance
Lightning Source LLC
Chambersburg PA
CBHW072039080526
44578CB00007B/520